D0603211

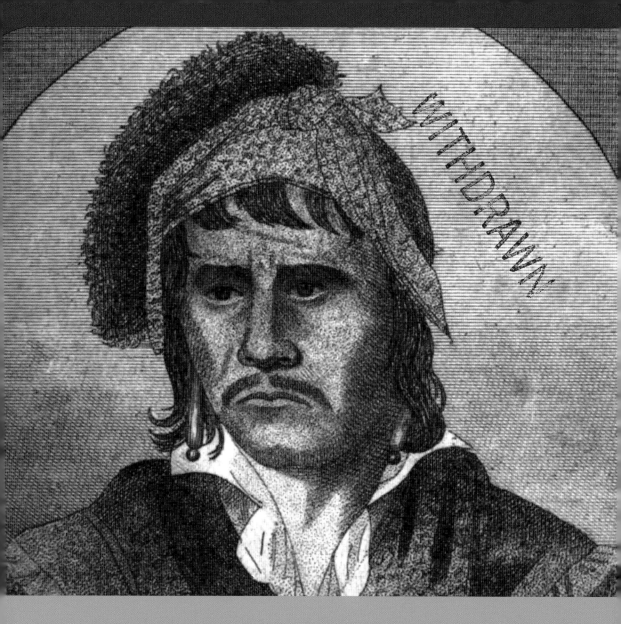

12 QUESTIONS ABOUT THE
INDIAN REMOVAL ACT

by Tracey E. Dils

STORY
LIBRARY

www.12StoryLibrary.com

12-Story Library is an imprint of Peterson Publishing Company and Press Room Editions.

Produced for 12-Story Library by Red Line Editorial

Photographs ©: Public Domain, cover, 1; fotoguy22/iStockphoto/Thinkstock, 4; John T. Bowen/Library of Congress, 5, 22, 28; North Wind Picture Archives, 6, 15; Photographs in the Carol M. Highsmith Archive/ Library of Congress, 7; Everett Historical/Shutterstock Images, 8, 20; wynnter/iStockphoto/Thinkstock, 9; GraphicaArtis/Corbis, 10; Henry S. Tanner/Corbis, 11; Carlo Gentile/Library of Congress, 12; Andrew_ Howe/iStock, 13; National Geographic Creative/Corbis, 16, 29; Gray & James/Library of Congress, 17; Library of Congress, 18, 23; nicoolay/iStockphoto, 19; Albert Newsam/Library of Congress, 21; SuperStock, 24; Sarah Cates/Shutterstock Images, 26, 27

Content Consultant: Dr. Greg O'Brien, PhD, Associate Professor, Department of History, University of North Carolina at Greensboro

Library of Congress Cataloging-in-Publication Data
Names: Dils, Tracey E., author.
Title: 12 questions about the Indian Removal Act / by Tracey E. Dils.
Other titles: Twelve questions about the Indian Removal Act
Description: Mankato, MN : 12-Story Library, 2017. | Series:
   Examining primary sources | Includes bibliographical references and index.
Identifiers: LCCN 2016002339 (print) | LCCN 2016002595 (ebook) | ISBN
   9781632352859 (library bound : alk. paper) | ISBN 9781632353351 (pbk. :
   alk. paper) | ISBN 9781621434528 (hosted ebook)
Subjects: LCSH: United States. Indian Removal Act of 1830. | Indian Removal,
   1813-1903. | Indians of North America--Government relations--1789-1869. |
   Cherokee Indians--Relocation.
Classification: LCC KF8203 1830 .D55 2016 (print) | LCC KF8203 1830 (ebook) |
   DDC 342.7308/72--dc23
LC record available at http://lccn.loc.gov/2016002339

Printed in the United States of America
Mankato, MN
May, 2016

Access free, up-to-date content on this topic plus a full digital version of this book. Scan the QR code on page 31 or use your school's login at 12StoryLibrary.com.

Table of Contents

What Happened after the American Revolution?

The United States had won its independence from Great Britain in 1783. The new country started to spread out beyond the original 13 colonies. In 1803, the United States bought a large area of land from France. This was called the Louisiana Purchase. The land was west of the Mississippi River. It stretched from the Gulf of Mexico to Canada. At the time, many people believed settlement would be driven by an idea that came to be known as Manifest Destiny. They felt that white settlers were destined to inhabit North America from coast to coast and from north to south.

But those who wanted to settle the Deep South were met with resistance. Approximately 60,000 American Indians lived in the South in the early 19th century. And they possessed nearly 20 million acres (8 million ha).

The American Indians who held this land were from several different tribes. They were mostly part of the Cherokee, Choctaw, Creek, Chickasaw, and Seminole tribes. They were called the "Civilized Tribes" by the US government, because some had taken on the ways of the white settlers. Some of the American Indians in the South could read and write in

5

Number of so-called "Civilized Tribes" in the United States in the early 1800s.

- Many American Indians lived in the southern United States.
- Some members of these tribes could read and write in English.
- The white settlers wanted to take over the land of these tribes.

CHEROKEE WRITING

Sequoyah was a Cherokee leader. He was convinced that the only way the Cherokees could survive was to have a written language. He began his work in 1809. By 1821, he had developed a way to convert the language into 86 symbols. This greatly increased the Cherokees' ability to communicate over long distances.

English. Some had their own written constitutions. Some owned slaves. Many had given up wearing their traditional clothing. They dressed as the settlers did. The Cherokees published their own newspaper called the *Cherokee Phoenix*. It was written in both the Cherokee language and English.

Sequoyah displays the Cherokee alphabet.

White people in Georgia, Alabama, and Mississippi wanted to claim the American Indians' land as their own. They wanted the land so they could grow crops, especially cotton. These settlers often struck out violently against the American

Indians. Some American Indians fought back. The battles caused bloodshed on both sides. The white settlers had superior weapons, so they usually won the battles.

GO TO THE SOURCE

To read the full text of the Indian Removal Act, go to **www.12StoryLibrary.com/primary**.

2

Why Did White People Want American Indians' Land?

White people wanted land for two important reasons. The most urgent was the hunger for gold. In 1829, gold was discovered on Cherokee land in what is now the state of Georgia. The Southern Gold Rush brought many white settlers to Cherokee territory. Miners wanted to claim the land where the gold was found.

But it was difficult to claim it when American Indians were living there.

The second reason was farming. The recent invention of the cotton gin made cotton a major cash crop. The soil in the South was rich. It was good for growing cotton and other crops. And the tribes had already developed the land. They had cleared fields. They had built fences. They had constructed buildings for their livestock. If the tribes left,

Prospectors pan for gold in Georgia in the 1800s.

Innovations in farming made cotton a popular crop in the South.

white farmers could use the farms as they were. They could start to grow crops immediately. That meant they could quickly profit from their farming by taking American Indian land.

The pressure was on to pave the way for the white settlers, who felt entitled to the land. This meant one thing: the American Indians would need to relocate. And the quicker, the better. The miners did not want the gold to run out. The farmers did not want to miss a growing season. They considered the matter urgent.

330
Weight, in pounds (150 kg), of gold that came from the mines in the Cherokee territory each day during the Southern Gold Rush.

- Gold was discovered on Cherokee land, bringing white miners to the area.
- White settlers wanted the farms the American Indians had already built.
- Pressure on the government to remove the American Indians grew stronger.

Whose Idea Was the Indian Removal Act?

Removing the American Indians from the South was an idea that had been long considered by the US government. Andrew Jackson, who was president at the time the act was passed, is often cited as the person behind the Indian Removal Act. He laid the groundwork for the law in his inaugural address. But Jackson wasn't the first to consider the idea. Thomas Jefferson had come up with a similar plan. Jefferson was

> Jefferson was an early proponent of relocating American Indians to the western United States.

THINK ABOUT IT

Jefferson came up with one way to move the American Indians from the South. After you read about Jackson's Indian Removal Act, compare the two plans. Which one do you think would have had a better outcome for the white settlers? Which one might have had a better outcome for the American Indians? In what ways? What might have happened if the US government had left the American Indians alone?

Monroe paved the way for the Indian Removal Act during his presidential term.

president from 1801 to 1809. His plan allowed the American Indians to sell their land to the United States. They could also leave their land to their heirs. The American Indians would then receive a parcel of land to the west where they could live and hunt.

In Jefferson's plan, the American Indians could not hunt if they chose to stay in the South. If they stayed, they also would have to become US citizens. American Indian tribes of the South resisted this plan. They considered the land theirs. They had

owned it before the white settlers arrived. They had lived there for thousands of years. Their right to the land had been recognized by treaties.

James Monroe, who was president from 1817 to 1825, had also backed the idea of American Indian removal. He spoke in support of it before he left office. The Seminole tribe battled US troops during Monroe's time in office. The war was fought on land that would become the state of Florida. At the time, Spain owned the land. When tensions with the Seminoles arose, Spain chose to sell the land to the United States.

What Was the Indian Removal Act of 1830?

The Indian Removal Act of 1830 gave President Jackson the right to negotiate treaties with the American Indian tribes of the southern states. The key word here is *negotiate*. The treaty did not require the white settlers and the American Indians to agree. It also did not clarify which terms had to be decided.

The treaties that followed the act promised the American Indians payment for their land if they agreed to sign. Nothing in either

Jackson was the US president from 1829 to 1837.

100,000

Approximate number of American Indians who would be moved to the West.

- The act allowed President Jackson to negotiate with the American Indians.
- The act did not say that the US government could use force to remove American Indians.
- Jackson himself benefitted financially from American Indian removal.

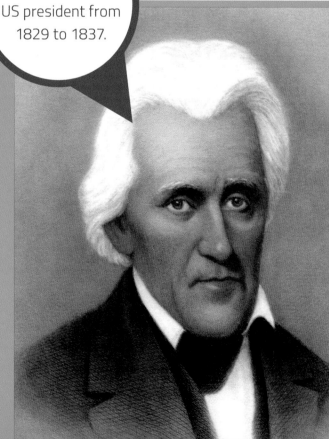

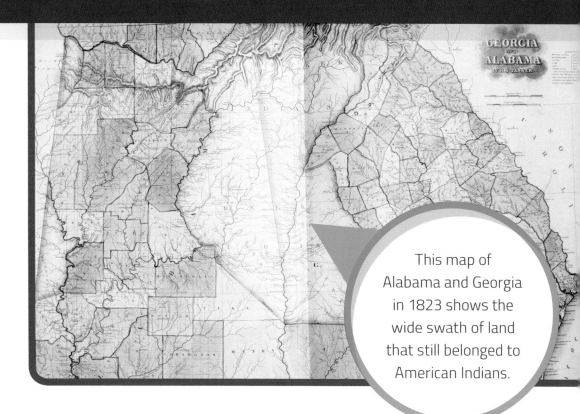

This map of Alabama and Georgia in 1823 shows the wide swath of land that still belonged to American Indians.

the act or the treaties indicated that the US government would use force to make the American Indians move west. Still, Jackson worked to make sure the move happened. He eventually moved 50,000 American Indians against their will from their homes in the South to new homes out west.

The white settlers were putting strong pressure on Jackson. These settlers wanted to move and profit from the riches of the South. In addition, Jackson himself was a land speculator. A land speculator is someone who buys property hoping to later sell it for a large profit. Some historians suggest that Jackson might have supported the Indian Removal Act because he wanted to enrich his own bank account as well.

THINK ABOUT IT

With the Indian Removal Act, Jackson could gain land for himself that he could sell for a profit. Was this fair? Can you think of any other ways that public figures or companies have made a profit by supporting new laws?

Did the Act Allow American Indians to Stay Behind?

Some treaties allowed American Indians to stay in the South. However, they had to give up their land and assimilate to white culture. This meant they had to dress, speak, and worship like the white settlers. They also had to give up their tribal nation status and become citizens of the United States.

Many American Indians had begun this process. Some had married white spouses. Even then, those who did stay and tried to fit in with the whites suffered. Many of these American Indians still found themselves victimized by the white settlers. The were forced to live in poverty and were shunned or attacked by the white people. Many ended up relocating after all to avoid this fate.

Two tribes, the Creeks and the Seminoles, decided they would fight back. This resulted in more warfare. The Creeks fought US troops over broken treaties in present-day Alabama in 1836. The Creeks were eventually defeated, and their survivors were forced west of the Mississippi River.

In order to be accepted by the white settlers, American Indians often had to give up many of their own traditional ways.

Some tribes fought back to maintain control of their land.

The Second Seminole War (1835–1842) lasted much longer. The Seminoles had some success fighting the US soldiers, who were not able to fight effectively in the swamps of Seminole territory, in present-day Florida. The Seminoles could easily hide in places such as the Everglades. They then surprised the soldiers with their attacks. But the power of the US troops eventually proved to be too much for the Seminoles. By the end of the war, most of them had been killed or relocated.

7

Number of years the Second Seminole War lasted.

- American Indians were allowed to stay in the South if they gave up their land and took on white customs and culture.
- Two tribes chose to fight to keep their land rather than move.
- The Seminoles had some success fighting US troops.

13

How Did the Indian Removal Act Pass?

President Jackson promoted a policy of moving the American Indians from their southern homes. He focused on the issue in his address when he was sworn into office in 1829. He wrote a number of messages to Congress justifying his actions. In these messages, he also focused on the positive outcomes of relocation. The American Indians would gain more land. They would not be bothered by their enemies or white settlers. More importantly, the white settlers would gain *their* valuable land. There was a sharp division and heated debate in Congress about removing the American Indians from their land. However, Jackson and his colleagues gathered enough support to pass the act.

The Cherokees wrote their own constitution in 1827. They believed they were adopting the ways of the settlers. But the white settlers did not see it that way. They did not want American Indians to form their own governments. They were viewed as a threat because it strengthened the Cherokees' claim to their land.

Because of this belief, the settlers tried to force the American Indians to follow state laws. The settlers who lived in southern states passed laws that were harmful to the

828,000
Amount of land, in square miles (2.1 million sq. km), in the Louisiana Purchase.

- White settlers in the South passed laws that hurt the American Indian population.
- The US government viewed the Cherokees' constitution as a threat.
- White people saw the Louisiana Purchase as a convenient place to move the American Indians.

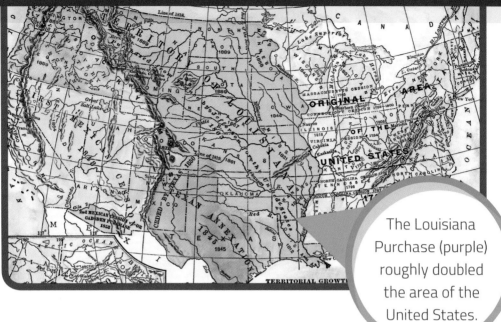

TERRITORIAL GROWTH

The Louisiana Purchase (purple) roughly doubled the area of the United States.

American Indians. These laws took away many rights, including their right to vote. One law suggested that American Indians could be killed if they were hostile to white settlers.

Jackson spoke of the successful passing of the act in his second annual address to Congress. He said, "It gives me pleasure to announce to Congress that the benevolent policy of the Government, steadily pursued for nearly 30 years, in relation to the removal of the Indians beyond the white settlements, is approaching to a happy consummation."

The Louisiana Purchase territory was a convenient place to move the American Indians. Before the US had acquired that land, there was no place to send American Indians. They either cooperated with the white settlers or waged war against them. The Louisiana Purchase made a large tract of land available west of the Mississippi River. Most white settlers and government officials saw this land as a convenient and adequate place to resettle the American Indians.

THINK ABOUT IT

If the United States had not made the Louisiana Purchase, what do you think might have happened to the American Indians who lived in the South? Why?

15

What Did the Act Provide American Indians?

The Indian Removal Act only promised one thing to American Indians: negotiation with the tribes to make the move west. The act said that the new territory in the West would belong to the American Indians forever. It said that the government could help the American Indians move and get settled in their new homes. It also promised that the American Indians would be protected from anyone who had already settled there. Individual contracts with each individual tribe specified other terms.

But the act was passed without consulting the tribes. The land west of the Mississippi River was far

Cherokee Indians forced to leave their homes on the Trail of Tears

Members of the Cherokee and Seminole tribes fought back against the forced relocation.

away from most of the American Indians' homelands. Worse still, they would have to walk hundreds of miles to their new homes. It was certainly not an even exchange for the land the American Indians had cultivated and developed. When some tribes, most notably the Cherokee and Seminole, did not comply, white Americans resorted to force to remove them from the land.

9
Number of states the Trail of Tears National Historic Trail crosses.

- The American government pledged to help the American Indians move.
- The land in the West was undeveloped and rugged.
- The American Indians were expected to walk to their new homes.

How Did the Southeastern American Indians Respond?

The Southeastern American Indians responded differently to the act. The Choctaws finalized their treaty with the US government in 1830. They were the first tribe to head west. The US government promised to help them move. But that help never came. Many Choctaws died on the journey due to exposure, malnutrition, exhaustion, and disease.

The Creeks did not want to move west. Their treaty allowed them to continue to live in what is now Alabama. But the citizens of Alabama made it impossible for the Creeks to stay. They raided their homes and their graves. The Creeks rose up in a war but were defeated by US soldiers. They eventually went west. But some escaped and returned to the area that is now the state of Florida.

The Chickasaws agreed to move. Instead of taking government money, the Chickasaw sold the land directly to white settlers. They used the money to head west. They took their belongings and their slaves with them.

Most of the Seminole tribe refused to move. Some, led by a chief named Neamathla, negotiated to

Neamathla

The tribes were herded to "Indian Territory," which later became Oklahoma.

remain in Florida on a reservation in the center of the state. But others fought back against settlers under their leader, Osceola. Most of the tribe was killed in battle or died from disease or starvation. The rest of the Seminoles moved west, except for a few hundred who were allowed to remain on an informal reservation in Florida.

The Cherokees put up the biggest fight. Some had adopted the ways of the white settlers. For the most part, they had cooperated. But a group of approximately 500 Cherokees betrayed their tribe. This group signed a treaty and agreed to move. Most of the tribe protested the group's decision. However, the tribe was eventually forced to accept the move west.

2,500
Estimated number of Choctaws who died on their journey west.

- The Creeks waged a war to stay in the South but were defeated.
- The Chickasaws sold their land themselves rather than take money from the government.
- Many in the Seminole tribe died, and most of the survivors moved west.

Who Opposed the Indian Removal Act?

The act created a great debate in and outside of Congress in the early part of Jackson's term. Its opponents said it violated the Constitution. They claimed the Constitution promised that treaties would be honored. These included the old treaties that gave the American Indians rights to their land in the South. Most of those opposed were political enemies of Jackson.

Outside the government, the act was also met with resistance. In a letter to Jackson, writer Ralph Waldo Emerson asked him to rethink the act. Many Christian missionaries also worked against it. They thought it was unfair and inhumane to take the American Indians' land.

Emerson was an active supporter of the antislavery movement as well.

Of course, most of the American Indians themselves were against the act because it would force them to leave their homeland. The Cherokees even brought the issue

Number of Supreme Court decisions that ruled in favor of the Cherokees.

- The Indian Removal Act faced opposition within and outside the government.
- President Jackson would not enforce the Supreme Court's decisions when it sided with the Cherokees.
- Jackson claimed that the Treaty of New Echota gave him the authority to move the Cherokees.

Jackson ignored the Supreme Court's ruling in favor of the Cherokees.

before the United States Supreme Court. They claimed the US government was in violation of previously signed treaties. Though the Supreme Court eventually sided with the Cherokees, its ruling had little effect. President Jackson refused to enforce it.

Jackson claimed that an earlier treaty, the Treaty of New Echota, showed that the Cherokees had accepted the move west. This treaty had been signed by a small number of Cherokees. None of the signers had been chosen by the tribe to represent it. Regardless, this treaty paved the way for American Indian removal.

Who Led the American Indian Resistance?

Some Cherokees chose to move, but the majority stayed behind under the leadership of John Ross. Ross's father was Scottish and his mother was part Cherokee. He was raised with the Cherokees. He encouraged the Cherokees to stay in their homeland but to take on the ways of the white settlers. He even modeled the Cherokee government after the US government.

But the settlers didn't really want the Cherokees to change their ways. They wanted the Cherokees to leave. Ross was imprisoned by the US government.

Ross wanted his fellow Cherokees to adapt to the culture of the white settlers.

2,000
Estimated number of Cherokees who voluntarily moved west.

- Most of the Cherokees stayed behind under Ross's leadership.
- After a forced march to what is now Oklahoma, Ross continued to lead the Cherokees.
- Osceola, a Seminole, led a war against US troops.

His home was taken from him. When the Cherokees were forced to move west, Ross led his people. His wife died during the journey. Once they arrived in what is now Oklahoma, he remained chief. He organized the Cherokees in their new home.

Osceola of the Seminole tribe was also a strong opponent of the move. Along with his tribe, he waged war upon the white soldiers. The Seminoles had the advantage of being able to hide effectively in the marshland of Florida. Then, the white men offered a truce to end the war. Osceola agreed and arranged a meeting. The meeting, though, was a trick. Osceola was captured and imprisoned. He spent the rest of his life in prison.

Osceola

WHO WAS OSCEOLA?

Osceola was a colorful figure among the Seminoles. He was known for being elegant in dress and handsome. He was also known for having a large ego. He was a fine speaker. He inspired his fellow Seminoles. When he was captured by the settlers through trickery, the world took notice. When he died in 1838 in prison, the news was carried in headlines all over the world. At the time of his death, Osceola was probably the most famous American Indian.

11

What Hardships Occurred on the Journey Westward?

The journey out of the South was difficult. The tribes traveled over rugged land. They crossed the wide, rushing Mississippi River. They suffered from malnutrition, exposure, exhaustion, and disease. They also fought off attacks by white settlers. Many of the displaced American Indians died along the way.

The Cherokees faced the most dramatic hardships. Many refused to leave their homeland in what is now Georgia. The military was brought in to force

The Trail of Tears was a brutal trek that cost many Cherokees their lives.

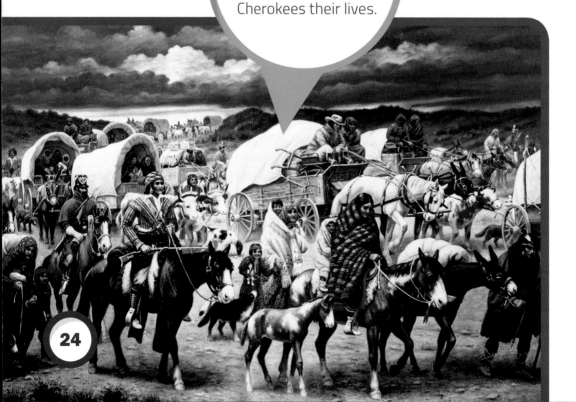

4,000

Estimated number of Cherokees who died along the Trail of Tears.

- The Cherokees were not allowed to collect their belongings.
- While the Cherokees were imprisoned, white settlers raided their homes.
- Some in bare feet, some in chains, the Cherokees marched to their new home in what is now Oklahoma.

their removal. The Cherokees were hunted down. Women were dragged from their houses. The Cherokees were not allowed to collect their belongings. Then, they were imprisoned until it was time to leave.

Once the Cherokees were gone, white settlers looted their homes. The settlers took whatever they thought was valuable. Then, they marched the Indians, some in chains, more than 1,200 miles (1,931 km) to Indian Territory west of the Mississippi River. Along the way, the Cherokees suffered

LIFE IN INDIAN TERRITORY

Once they arrived in the new Indian Territory, the American Indians returned to farming. They were very successful at first. Then, the US Civil War (1861–1865) broke out. Because the tribes were living in an area bordered by free and slave states, their territory became a centerpiece of conflict. They were attacked by both the Union and Confederate armies. Their crops were stolen. Many of their buildings were burned. Life in Indian Territory was anything but the peaceful refuge they had been promised.

terribly from disease. Whooping cough, typhus, dysentery, and cholera spread throughout the travelers. The US government did not prepare well for the trip. The soldiers did not bring enough food. Many of the Cherokees suffered from starvation as well. The journey was so tragic that it has become known as the "Trail of Tears."

How Is the Indian Removal Act Viewed Today?

Today, the Indian Removal Act is viewed as a regrettable part of US history. The American Indians who died on the way to the West underwent unspeakable hardships. Many who successfully made it to the new territory were not comfortable with their new setting. It carried none of the traditions and emotional connection

A woman dances at the annual Trail of Tears powwow.

5.2 million

Number of people of American Indian or Alaskan heritage living in the United States, according to the 2010 Census.

- The Indian Removal Act is seen as a dark part of American history.
- The American Indians who went west suffered extreme hardships.
- Festivals and powwows help remind us of the Indian Removal Act.

An American Indian man wears traditional clothing during the annual Trail of Tears powwow.

that their native land had provided.

Today, the five Southeastern tribes are featured in memorials and festivals. Perhaps the most well-known is the Cherokee National Holiday. It is celebrated in Tahlequah, Oklahoma, every Labor Day weekend. Traditional dances and music are performed. Traditional food is also served. The Seminoles also have a headquarters in Hollywood, Florida. Every year, they have a tribal fair and powwow. These events and others are celebrations. But they also serve as a reminder of the dark times of the Indian Removal Act.

Fact Sheet

- The Louisiana Purchase was made in 1803 at less than three cents an acre. The purchase doubled the size of the United States.

- In the years after the Indian Removal Act, white people pushed westward. Some American Indians lost some or all of their land.

- Sequoyah developed a written form of the Cherokee language with his daughter. The alphabet was based on English, Greek, and Hebrew. A statue of Sequoyah can be found at the US Capitol, the first of any American Indian to be enshrined in the National Statuary Hall.

- Congress made the Trail of Tears a National Historic Trail in 1987. The trail is dedicated to those who died or were injured along the way. It is one of 19 National Historic Trails established by the US government between 1978 and 2009. All told, the Trail of Tears National Historic Trail encompasses 2,200 miles (3,500 km) and crosses or touches the border of nine states in the southeastern United States.

Glossary

adopt
Take on as one's own.

assimilate
To fully become part of a different society or culture.

civilized
Improved as a culture or society; to be better organized.

debate
An argument or discussion among people who have different opinions on a subject.

gold rush
A period when many people move to an area hoping to find gold.

livestock
Animals that are raised to make a profit for their owners.

loot
To steal in a riot or a war.

Manifest Destiny
A belief held by many in the 1800s that white US settlers were destined to spread throughout North America.

memorial
An event or place that honors a time in history.

negotiate
To discuss in search of a solution to a problem.

For More Information

Books

Schwartz, Heather E. *Forced Removal: Causes and Effects of the Trail Of Tears.* North Mankato, MN: Capstone Press, 2015.

Walker, Paul Robert. *American Indians.* New York: Kingfisher, 2011.

Yomtov, Nel. *Andrew Jackson: Heroic Leader or Cold-Hearted Ruler?* North Mankato, MN: Capstone Press, 2014.

Visit 12StoryLibrary.com

Scan the code or use your school's login at **12StoryLibrary.com** for recent updates about this topic and a full digital version of this book. Enjoy free access to:

- Digital ebook
- Breaking news updates
- Live content feeds
- Videos, interactive maps, and graphics
- Additional web resources

Note to educators: Visit 12StoryLibrary.com/register to sign up for free premium website access. Enjoy live content plus a full digital version of every 12-Story Library book you own for every student at your school.

Index

About the Author

Tracey E. Dils is the author of more than 40 books for young readers. She has been awarded the Ohioana Award in Children's Literature. Tracey graduated from the College of Wooster in Wooster, Ohio, and lives with her husband in Columbus, Ohio.

READ MORE FROM 12-STORY LIBRARY

Every 12-Story Library book is available in many formats. For more information, visit 12StoryLibrary.com.